Great Americans

Sam Houston

Barbara Kiely Miller

Reading consultant: Susan Nations, M.Ed., author/literacy coach/
consultant in literacy development

WEEKLY READER
PUBLISHING

Please visit our web site at: **www.garethstevens.com**
For a free color catalog describing our list of high-quality books,
call 1-800-542-2595 (USA) or 1-800-387-3178 (Canada).

Library of Congress Cataloging-in-Publication Data

Kiely Miller, Barbara.
  Sam Houston / by Barbara Kiely Miller.
    p. cm. — (Great Americans)
  Includes bibliographical references and index.
  ISBN-13: 978-0-8368-8316-9 (lib. bdg.)
  ISBN-13: 978-0-8368-8323-7 (softcover)
  ISBN-10: 0-8368-8316-0 (lib. bdg.)
  ISBN-10: 0-8368-8323-3 (softcover)
  1. Houston, Sam, 1793–1863—Juvenile literature. 2. Governors—Texas—
Biography—Juvenile literature. 3. Legislators—United States—Biography—
Juvenile literature. 4. United States. Congress. Senate—Biography—Juvenile
literature. 5. Texas—History—To 1846—Juvenile literature. I. Title.
  F390.H84K54   2008
  976.4'04'092—dc22   2007008100

This edition first published in 2008 by
Weekly Reader® Books
An imprint of Gareth Stevens Publishing
1 Reader's Digest Road
Pleasantville, NY 10570-7000 USA

Copyright © 2008 by Gareth Stevens, Inc.

Managing editor: Valerie J. Weber
Art direction: Tammy West
Cover design and page layout: Charlie Dahl
Picture research: Sabrina Crewe
Production: Jessica Yanke

Picture credits: Cover, title page, p. 11 The Granger Collection, New York; p. 5 Sam
Houston Memorial Museum; p. 6 © David Muench/Corbis; pp. 7, 8, 10, 13, 17 Texas State
Library and Archives Commission; p. 14 Dave Kowalski and Charlie Dahl/© Gareth Stevens,
Inc.; p. 15 Courtesy of the State Preservation Board, Austin, Texas, CHA 1989.90, painting
by Henry McArdle, photograph by Perry Huston; p. 16 © Bettmann/Corbis; p. 19 © Getty
Images; p. 20 Charlie Dahl/© Gareth Stevens, Inc.; p. 21 photo courtesy of Top City
Photos www.top-city-photos.com.

Table of Contents

Chapter 1: From Farmer to Hero 4

Chapter 2: A Leader for Tennessee 9

Chapter 3: Fighting for Texas's Independence 12

Chapter 4: Texas Becomes a State 18

Glossary 22

For More Information 23

Index 24

Cover and title page: Sam Houston was the governor of both Tennessee and Texas. He fought for Texas's independence from Mexico — and won!

Chapter 1

From Farmer to Hero

Sam Houston sat straight and tall on his horse, ready to attack. He was the leader of eight hundred men. His small Texas army was about to face almost twice as many Mexican soldiers. Texas's freedom from Mexico depended on who won the battle.

The Mexicans did not see the Texans approach, and with their surprise attack, the little army won the battle. Texas was now a free **republic**. Sam Houston would soon be its first president.

After Texas became part of the United States, Houston also served in **Congress** and as the state's governor. He is remembered most, however, as the leader who won Texas its freedom.

Houston led his soldiers into battle. He told them they had to attack the larger Mexican army or give up all hope of independence.

The Houston family moved to a farm like this one in eastern Tennessee. Although his older brothers liked farming, Sam Houston wanted more adventure.

Samuel Houston was born March 2, 1793, near Lexington, Virginia. He had five brothers and three sisters. Their father was a soldier. He died when Houston was thirteen years old. Soon after his death, their mother moved the family to a farm in Tennessee.

Sam Houston did not want to be a farmer. When he was fifteen years old, he ran away to live with a group of Cherokee Indians. After three years, Houston went home. He would stay friends with the Cherokees, however, for the rest of his life. He would work to help them and other Native Americans.

Sam Houston lived with Chief Oolooteka (*left*) and his Cherokee people. The chief thought of Sam as his own son.

In 1813, Houston turned twenty. The United States was at war with Great Britain. Houston joined the U.S. Army to fight the Creek Indians, who were helping the British. Houston was a brave and skilled soldier. In a battle in 1814, however, he was badly wounded.

After he was hit by an arrow, Houston asked another solider to pull it out so he could keep fighting.

Chapter 2

A Leader for Tennessee

In 1818, Houston became a lawyer in Nashville, Tennessee. Five years later, the people of Tennessee elected him as their **representative** in Congress. He spent four years making laws in the nation's capital.

Sam Houston liked helping the people of his state. In 1827, when he was thirty-four, he was elected governor of Tennessee. Houston only kept the job for two years, however. In 1829, he went back to live with his Cherokee family, who now lived in eastern Oklahoma.

This picture of Houston was painted when he was in Congress. As a congressman, Houston often spoke out about the mistreatment of the Cherokees.

The U.S. government had forced the Cherokees to give up their land and move. Their new land, however, was smaller than the area that the government had promised them. The government had not paid money it owed them either. Houston worked to get the Cherokees treated more fairly.

Houston's Cherokee friends moved to Oklahoma in 1818. Twenty years later, the government forced Cherokees in Georgia to move there, too. Thousands of them died during the long trip.

Chapter 3

Fighting for Texas's Independence

After three years with the Cherokees, Sam Houston moved to Texas in 1832. Texas was a state of Mexico then, but thousands of people from the United States had settled there. These settlers were called Anglos. Many Anglos did not want to obey Mexico's laws. Houston and others thought Texas should fight for freedom from Mexico.

Houston became the military leader for the town of Nacogdoches. On March 2, 1836, he met with other Texan leaders. The men signed the Texas **Declaration of Independence**, which said Texas would no longer belong to Mexico. They also wrote the **constitution** for the Republic of Texas. It gave Texas new laws of its own. The men also picked Houston to head its army.

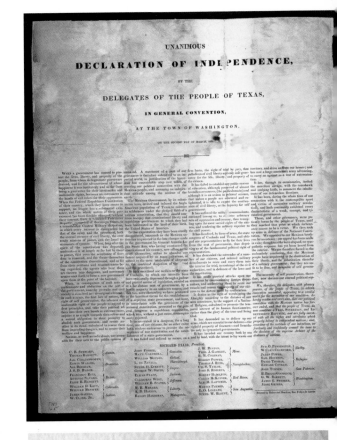

The men who signed Texas's Declaration of Independence represented all of its towns. Sam Houston's name is in the column on the right.

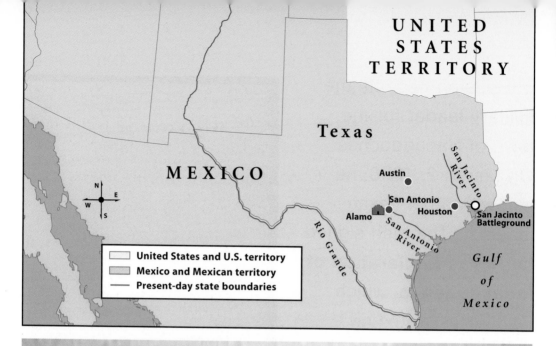

Texas and the rest of the area colored in orange were once part of Mexico. Part of the Alamo still stands in San Antonio.

Mexico's leader was Antonio Lopéz de Santa Anna. He wanted to keep Texas part of Mexico. Santa Anna had an army of four thousand men. On March 6, 1836, he attacked an Anglo fort in San Antonio called the Alamo. Fewer than three hundred men were inside the fort. They fought bravely, but all of them died.

With only eight hundred soldiers, Sam Houston chased Santa Anna and his army. On April 21, Houston found him and fourteen hundred soldiers camped along the San Jacinto River. The Texans attacked, shouting, "Remember the Alamo." The battle lasted only twenty minutes. Houston had won! Only six Anglo men died, while over six hundred Mexican soldiers were killed.

This painting of the Battle of San Jacinto was completed in 1895. Houston is shown in the middle of the picture standing next to a Mexican canon and waving his hat.

Santa Anna (*bowing*) surrendered to Sam Houston after being captured. Later, he was allowed to return to Mexico.

During the battle, Houston was shot in the ankle. He rested the next day, while his soldiers captured Santa Anna. The Mexican leader told Houston that he would stop fighting. Houston had done it — he had won independence for Texas! It was now a separate nation.

Houston served as the first and third president of the new Republic of Texas. He also stopped Mexico when it tried to take back Texas.

Texans named a new city after him. Houston would be Texas's capital for the next two years.

This cabin in the city of Houston served as the president's house. The city of Austin later became the capital of the Republic of Texas and of the state of Texas.

Chapter 4

Texas Becomes a State

In 1840, Sam Houston got married. He and his wife Margaret had four sons and four daughters.

On December 29, 1845, Texas became a state and joined the United States. Houston became one of Texas's two senators. He was elected two more times and served in Washington, D.C., from 1846 to 1859.

Houston often had different ideas than other congressmen. He had **slaves** and did not think slavery should end. But Houston also thought that new areas that wanted to join the United States should not have slavery. Many people, especially in the northern states, thought slavery anywhere was wrong.

For twenty-five years, Sam Houston served the people of Texas as a government leader.

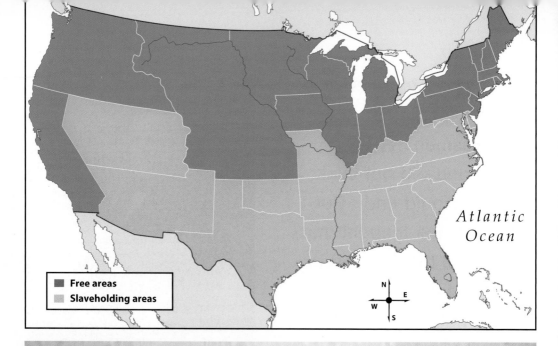

Atlantic
Ocean

Free areas
Slaveholding areas

N
E
W
S

This map shows which parts of the United States allowed slavery and which parts did not. Disagreements about slavery led to the U.S. Civil War.

In December 1859, Houston became governor of Texas. In 1861, Texas and other southern states split from the northern states and set up their own government. They did not want to give up slavery. Houston knew that this separation would lead to war and that the more powerful North would win.

Houston stayed loyal to the northern government. On March 16, 1861, Texans made him give up his job as governor. One month later, the Civil War began. Houston and his family moved to Huntsville, Texas. He died there on July 26, 1863. Sam Houston is the only person in U.S. history to be governor of two different states. Most importantly, he is the Texan hero who defeated a huge army and won freedom.

This statue of Sam Houston in Huntsville, Texas, is the world's tallest statue of an American hero.

Glossary

Anglos — white, English-speaking people who are not Hispanic

capital — the city where a state's or country's government is located

Civil War — the American war fought between Northern and Southern states from 1861 to 1865

Congress — the part of the United States government that makes laws. The people in Congress are called representatives and senators.

constitution — a piece of writing that states how a country will be governed

Declaration of Independence — a statement in which people declare their freedom from another country

governor — a person who governs, or rules, a state

lawyer — a person whose job is to give legal advice and to represent people in court

representative — someone who is elected or chosen to act for others

republic — a country in which the people elect their own lawmakers

slaves — people who are treated as property and are forced to work without pay. Slaves do not have freedom.

For More Information

Books

The Alamo. Places in American History (series). Frances E. Ruffin (Gareth Stevens Publishing)

L is for Lone Star: A Texas Alphabet. Carol Crane (Sleeping Bear Press)

Sam Houston. First Biographies (series). Lisa Trumbauer (Capstone Press)

Sam Houston. What's So Great About . . . ? (series). Susan Sales Harkins and William H. Harkins (Mitchell Lane Publishers)

Web Sites

Harcourt Multimedia Biographies: Sam Houston
www.harcourtschool.com/activity/biographies/houston
Read another story about Sam Houston's life.

Sam Houston Memorial Museum
www.shsu.edu/~smm_www
See a time line of Sam Houston's life and photos of his family.

Publisher's note to educators and parents: Our editors have carefully reviewed these Web sites to ensure that they are suitable for children. Many Web sites change frequently, however, and we cannot guarantee that a site's future contents will continue to meet our high standards of quality and educational value. Be advised that children should be closely supervised whenever they access the Internet.

Index

Alamo 14, 15
armies 4, 5, 8, 13, 14, 15, 21
Austin 17

Battle of San Jacinto 15
battles 4, 5, 8, 15, 16

Civil War 20, 21
Congress 5, 9, 10, 18, 19

families 6, 7, 18, 21
farming 6, 7

freedom 4, 5, 12, 16, 21

governors 5, 10, 20, 21

Houston, city of 17

Mexico 4, 12, 13, 14, 16, 17

Native Americans 7, 8, 10, 11, 12

presidents 5, 17

Republic of Texas 5, 13, 17

Santa Anna, Antonio Lopéz de 14, 15, 16
senators 18
settlers 12
slavery 19, 20
soldiers 4, 5, 8, 6, 15

Tennessee 6, 9, 10
Texas 4, 5, 12, 13, 14, 17, 18, 20, 21

United States 5, 8, 11, 12, 18, 19

About the Author

Barbara Kiely Miller is an editor and writer of educational books for children. She has a degree in creative writing from the University of Wisconsin–Milwaukee. Barbara lives in Shorewood, Wisconsin, with her husband and their two cats Ruby and Sophie. When she is not writing or reading books, Barbara enjoys photography, bicycling, and gardening.